VANISHING HABITATS

ISBN 0-531-17062-4

Library of Congress Catalog
Card Number: 87-80458

Printed in Belgium

Designed and produced by
Aladdin Books Ltd
70 Old Compton Street
London W1

First published in the
United States in 1987 by
Gloucester Press
387 Park Avenue South
New York, NY 10016

The front cover photograph shows a devastated rain forest in Brazil.
The back cover photograph shows squirrel monkeys in the forest.

The author, Noel Simon, worked for the International Union for
Conservation of Nature and Natural Resources in Switzerland. He
compiled the Mammalia volume of the Red Data Book, the
international catalogue of the world's rare and endangered species.
He is also the author of many children's books on Natural History.

The consultant, Michael Bright, is a Senior Producer at the BBC's
Natural History Unit, Bristol, UK. He is also author of several books
on Natural History.

Contents

VANISHING HABITATS

Noel Simon

Gloucester Press

New York : London : Toronto : Sydney

Introduction

Habitat is the area in which a particular plant or animal lives, the place where the essential conditions for its life exist. A healthy habitat is a basic necessity: it provides air to breathe, water to drink and food to eat. But air and water are being polluted and habitats being ruined. The squandering of Earth's natural resources is creating an increasingly ravaged world. And since animals and plants live in a delicate balance with their habitat, the decaying of this habitat is a great threat to their survival.

Much of the damage to habitat results from the increasing numbers of people. In the third world 500 million people are underfed and 800 million suffer poverty. To simply stay alive and avoid starvation, these people are degrading their habitat still further by cutting down forests, by overstocking their grazing lands and by cultivating unsuitable land. In the industrial world, habitats are being degraded by pollution and commercial exploitation.

This book looks at the main types of large-scale habitats found in the world, as well as at some smaller examples, and shows what is happening to them. It also points out that the degradaton of habitat poses a threat to the quality of life and ultimately to human survival.

◁◁ Each increase in human numbers adds to the growing pressures on habitat and natural resources. The rain forests (far left) are destroyed through timber extraction, burning and grazing.

◁ Squirrel monkeys (left) are widely distributed in the rain forests of South America. They feed on lizards, eggs and insects. Animals like these are under threat from the destruction of the rain forests.

The vanishing forests

By the year 2000, one third of the world's tropical rain forest will have been destroyed. Almost half of this rain forest lies in Brazil. It has had an extremely high rate of growth and a varied plant and animal life. Amazonia, for instance, possesses one million species of plants and animals. When the trees are cut down, leaving the ground exposed, the plant nutrients are quickly washed out of the soil. The land then becomes unproductive. As most tropical rain forests grow on sterile soil, this process happens quickly. Replanting of trees seldom takes place. Even when it does, quick-growing pines or eucalyptus are usually planted instead of tropical rain forest trees.

Often the forests – which contain valuable hardwoods such as teak and mahogany – are seen only as an endless source of timber for logging and fuel. The timber industry has expanded greatly in the last 30 years and some forests, particularly in Southeast Asia, have been so exploited that they have been ruined.

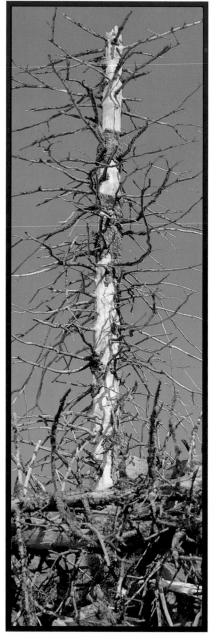

▽ The photograph shows the effects of acid rain. Poisonous gases from factory smoke-stacks and car exhausts are carried by winds and fall to earth in the form of acid rain. Forests, lakes and rivers in more than 20 industrialized countries are affected. Half of Switzerland's forests are already dying.

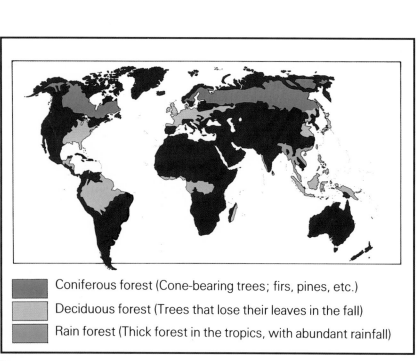

■ Coniferous forest (Cone-bearing trees; firs, pines, etc.)

■ Deciduous forest (Trees that lose their leaves in the fall)

■ Rain forest (Thick forest in the tropics, with abundant rainfall)

The largest stretch of coniferous forest in the world – the taiga – encircles the earth in the northern hemisphere. The taiga supplies the bulk of the world's commercial softwood timber. The dominant tree species is larch, but fir, spruce and others are common. Coniferous forest reaches down North America's Pacific coast to California. Some of the world's mightiest trees – Douglas firs, redwoods and sequoias – are found in this area. The greatest threat to coniferous forest comes from acid rain. Huge areas are affected.

Deciduous forest used to cover much of Europe and the whole of the eastern part of North America. Most of it has been destroyed. What is left of the deciduous forest today, however, is well preserved, especially in the United States. Typical species are oak, beech, ash and chestnut.

In Europe's deciduous forests, animals such as the wild boar, red fox, roe deer, badger and squirrel are common. Typical North American species are the white-tailed deer and wild turkey.

△ Tawny owl

▷ A deciduous tree forms the habitat for many kinds of animals. But because of differences in feeding habits and behavior, the various species do not conflict with one another. Some birds, for example, specialize in eating either insects, seeds or fruit.

On the forest floor, decaying leaves and rotting branches provide food for huge numbers of insects. Badgers dig rodents from their burrows, while deer feed on grass, leaves and shoots. Foxes, weasels, hawks and owls prey upon mice, voles, rats and rabbits. The purple emperor butterfly usually spends most of its life in the tops of oak trees. Together, the animals and their habitat form a balanced system – an ecosystem.

△ Purple emperor butterfly

Rain forests

Destruction of habitat is the single greatest threat to the survival of species. Safeguarding different types of habitat is therefore the most effective measure that can be taken to conserve them. Many rare species – such as the Javan rhinoceros – have survived only because a national park has been created for them. Other animals such as the orangutan, which lives in the tropical forests of Borneo and Sumatra, are more likely to be endangered.

Emergent

Swift

Harpy eagle

Canopy

Hummingbird

Toucan

Marmoset

Middle

Morphos butterfly

Scarlet macaw

Emerald tree boa

Understory

Arrow frog

Jaguar

Tarantula

Forest floor

△ Birds of paradise are found only in the forests of New Guinea and nearby islands. They form the most brilliantly colored group of birds in the world.

◁ The forest canopy is made up of three or more layers. Each consists of the crowns of different types of trees and supports different types of the understory. The middle story, the canopy, reaches to about 36 m (118 ft.). Towering above all else is the top (emergent) layer, reaching to about 45 m (148 ft.). In the Amazonian forests large mammals such as the tapir and the jaguar are confined to the forest floor. The pygmy anteater and the tamandua climb the trees in search of the termites and insects. The canopy supports a wealth of brightly plumaged birds.

Great Indian Rhino

Javan Rhino

Sumatran Rhino

△ The Javan rhino is extremely rare. Its last remaining stronghold is the Udjong Kulon Reserve on the western tip of Java, where there are about 40 individual animals.

Their reproduction rate is low and fears have been expressed that there are not enough births to compensate for losses. The male has one horn — the female none.

△ The Javan and Sumatran rhinos live in dense forest, browsing along the edge of clearings; the Indian rhino prefers swampy jungle, feeding on grass and reeds.

◁ The orangutan is the only one of the great apes to be found outside Africa. It lives in the tropical forest of Borneo and Sumatra and finds it difficult to adapt to any other type of habitat. Loss of habitat, both for logging and to provide more cultivated land for the ever-expanding human population, is splitting the remaining orangutans into small and often isolated groups, which have greater difficulty in surviving.

The grasslands

The four major grassland regions in the world, the North American prairie, the South American pampas, the Eurasian steppe, and the African savanna have all been intensively exploited and developed. The prairies of North America were very suitable for cattle ranching and wheat growing. Thousands of acres were plowed, and thousands more overstocked and overgrazed. Removal of the natural grass cover exposed the soil to the hot sun, causing it to dry out, become sandy, and be blown away by the high winds. Today, soil erosion is sometimes controlled by contour plowing, a technique that prevents the soil being blown or washed away from exposed hillsides.

The vast steppe lands of Central Asia have also been used for cattle ranching and agriculture. The herds of gazelles, wild Bactrian camels, wild asses and wild horses that used to live there have been reduced. They were destroyed partly by unrestricted hunting and partly because the nomads prevented the wild herds from having access to scarce water which they wanted for their own domestic livestock.

The photograph shows bison, or buffalo, one of the animals closely associated with the prairie. The settlement and development of the prairie a century ago marked the end not only of the buffalo but also of the Plains Indians whose way of life was closely tied up with the buffalo. Within a few decades the immense buffalo herds, estimated to have once numbered 60 million, had been largely destroyed. When survivors were discovered in Canada, Wood Buffalo Park was established for their protection.

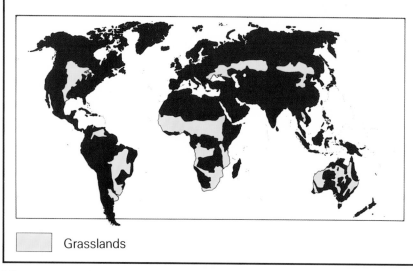

☐ Grasslands

An animal carcass in Africa is one of the symbols of the expanding deserts. Areas of dry grassland unsuited for agriculture are used by nomads and their herds of domestic animals. As numbers steadily increase, overgrazing becomes inevitable. The fragile vegetation is destroyed and the deserts encroach on cattle, sheep and goats. Starvation follows.

"While our prairie grain belt is of great importance to North America no one will ever again see the ecosystem of the grassland that existed there before the white man's settlement."

Charles Caccia
Minister of the
Environment,
Canada, 1984

The desert

Until recently, deserts were regarded by many people as wastelands and were therefore natural safe places or sanctuaries. But the discovery of oil brought dramatic changes. Lands considered useless quickly became among the richest, for beneath them there is an enormous wealth of oil. However, this oil wealth has opened up the deserts to every kind of exploitation. Often, the oil crews relieve their boredom by hunting any wild animals they can find. Poor nomads on horse or camel and rich Arabs in motorized cavalcades have added to the toll. The addax and the slender-horned gazelle, once among the most common animals in the Sahara, have become very rare. In Arabia the ostrich, bustard and cheetah have been exterminated and three species of gazelle are almost gone. The Arabian oryx was saved from extinction only by capturing the last few survivors.

Deserts are another example of how a habitat can gradually be degraded. And because animals are linked together by food chains, the downfall of one species quickly leads to serious survival problems for another.

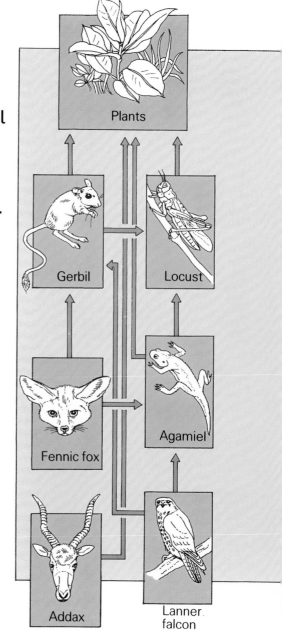

Plants

Gerbil

Locust

Fennic fox

Agamiel

Addax

Lanner falcon

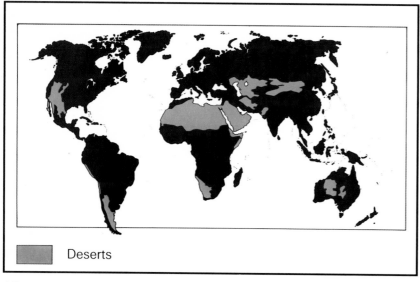

Deserts

△ The base of the desert food chain is formed of numerous insects feeding on plants. Insects are eaten by spiders, scorpions and their small predators, gerbils. Lizards feed on locusts and are themselves the prey of snakes and hawks. Lizards are eaten by the fennic fox which also feeds on gerbils. At the top of the food chain are the big predators, which prey on the large grass-eaters, such as the addax.

"In the name of progress the ecosystems of the third world
are daily subjected to torments from the most sophisticated
technologies."

Felipe Benavides, Peruvian ex-Diplomat

The Kalahari Desert has only sparse vegetation but the recent expansion of Botswana's cattle industry has greatly increased the numbers of livestock using the area. Long lines of fences have been constructed to control the spread of disease. These fences cut across the traditional migratory routes followed by the herds of wildebeest, zebra, eland, springbok and other species in search of winter grazing and water. Their routes blocked, the wild animals die of starvation and thirst on the wire fences. Losses have been on a huge scale.

△ The addax lives in waterless and uninhabited country deep in the Sahara, and thus does not compete either with humans or domestic livestock. Properly managed, the addax could be a valuable source of protein. Instead, it has been nearly exterminated.

The cold wilderness

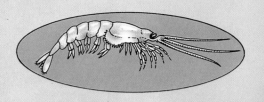

Antarctica, covering more than 12 million sq km (4.6 million sq mi), is the only continent entirely without a human population. Unpolluted and unexploited, it forms the perfect wildlife sanctuary. The Antarctic Treaty, signed in 1959, outlawed commercial exploitation of Antarctica. Human activities were restricted to genuine scientific work. But valuable oil and other mineral deposits are known to exist there and demands are already being made to allow their exploitation.

△ Fishing for krill – a shrimp-like animal of high protein value – is being massively increased. Krill is a key animal in Antarctica's ecosystem as it is the main food for baleen whales and many seabirds.

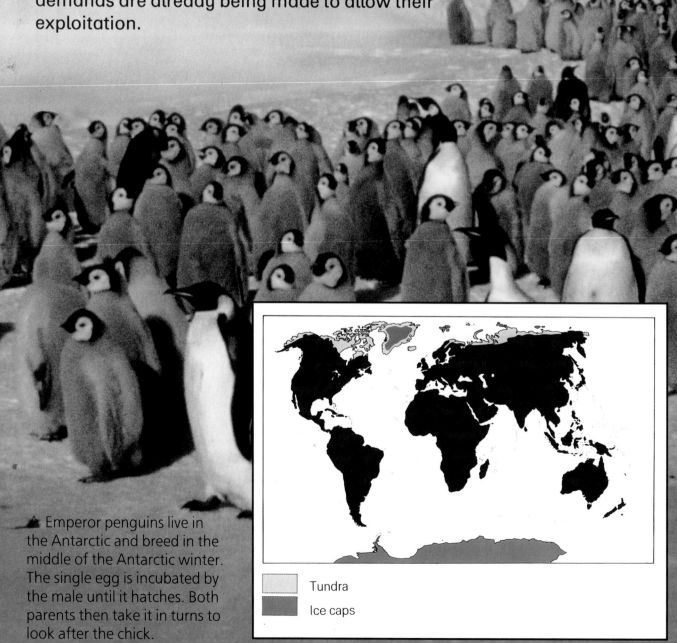

△ Emperor penguins live in the Antarctic and breed in the middle of the Antarctic winter. The single egg is incubated by the male until it hatches. Both parents then take it in turns to look after the chick.

Tundra
Ice caps

...the tundra

The tundra is the largest continuous tract of wilderness and wildlife habitat remaining in the northern hemisphere. But, in 1968, with the discovery of oil near Prudhoe Bay, in Alaska, technology burst upon it. The installation of a 1,300 km (800 mile) long pipeline, the sinking of wells, road construction and the movement of heavy equipment created ecological disturbance over a wide area.

In summer the surface of the tundra thaws, leaving the land studded with pools, lakes and marshes. Mosquitoes, midges and blackflies hang above the tundra like a dark mist. Migrant birds come by the millions, attracted by the insect food and the secure refuge. Ducks and geese find rich pastures in the extensive wetlands. Almost constant daylight allows maximum time for feeding – ideal conditions for raising nestlings. More than 100 migrant bird species nest on the tundra, making it the most important bird sanctuary in the world.

△ The photograph shows a new tundra highway carefully built to avoid unnecessary damage to the habitat. The tundra consists of two layers, the top layer which is frozen in winter but thaws in summer and the permafrost layer – which is always frozen. Frozen soils are particularly vulnerable to disturbance, and the use of tracked vehicles on the tundra during spring and summer creates gullies, causing soil erosion. This leaves behind permanent scars. The diagram shows how even slight tracks can deepen once the frozen topsoil begins to melt.

SURVIVAL PROFILE...

Arctic life

For thousands of years the Arctic has remained an unspoiled natural sanctuary. But severe climatic conditions are no longer being allowed to stand in the way of development. The northern territories are being opened up for both military and industrial purposes. Exploration, research and development are governed by military requirements such as early warning systems and air bases. The Arctic's mineral wealth is also being exploited.

The polar bear
Male polar bears may be 5 ft high at the shoulder and weigh 1,000 lbs. Their broad feet have furry soles with the front paws partially webbed. Cubs (usually twins) are born in dens in the ice. Newborn cubs weigh less than 2 lbs.

△ There are about 10,000 polar bears, mostly in the Canadian Arctic. Much of the polar bear's life is spent at sea among the pack ice: it is an expert swimmer. Its main prey is the ringed seal. In summer when the ice breaks up and seals become scarce, the polar bear moves ashore. Summer is a lean period for the polar bear. Hunger drives it to eat anything it can find – carrion, seaweed, berries, birds' eggs – or even to raid garbage cans and dumps. Apart from subsistence hunting by Eskimos, the species is protected over most of its range. Pollution from off-shore oil drilling and spillage from pipe lines are a danger, but an even more sinister threat comes from the accumulation of lethal quantities of poisonous chemicals in the bears' bodies. These chemicals come from the seals on which they prey mainly during the winter.

△ The caribou – the same animal as the domesticated reindeer of the Lapps and other Arctic peoples – undergoes a seasonal migration into the tundra. In April the herds of barren ground caribou, together with their newborn calves, leave their wintering grounds in northern Canada and trek northwards across the tundra, feeding as they go on the reindeer moss uncovered by the melting snow. After summering in high latitudes and mating during September, the herds – sometimes assembling in groups of several thousand – start the return journey to their winter quarters. The migrating herds of caribou are followed by packs of wolves which prey on stragglers and on the sick members of the herd.

The caribou
Males stand 4 ft at the shoulder (females are smaller) and weigh up to 600 lbs. Both sexes have antlers. Broad, flat hooves are an adaptation for walking on wetlands and snow. Females produce a single calf after 8 months' gestation.

▷ Both caribou and reindeer have been affected by radioactive fallout, the latter from the accident at the nuclear power plant in Chernobyl, USSR. The reindeer moss (seen in the photograph) on which they feed accumulates radioactive substances which become concentrated in their bodies.

Mountain sanctuaries

People have long been attracted by the beauty of high mountains and tourism has become big business. Getting tourists into the Alps has meant the building of roads and railroads, ski-lifts and resorts.

Other man-made developments have affected the habitat. Huge dams have been built to store water from melted snow to be used for irrigation or hydroelectric power. Because intensive development in the lowlands wiped out many of Europe's native predators, the mountains have become the last stronghold for some of the world's rarest fauna. The golden eagle, the wild cat and the lynx are now almost entirely confined to the more remote mountains.

▷ The alpine ibex lives on cliffs and crags close to the snow line and is astonishingly sure-footed. A century ago the ibex was almost exterminated by hunting. The only survivors were a few in a remote part of the Italian Alps, from which the animal was later reintroduced into Switzerland, France, Austria and Yugoslavia.

"Man is tinkering with his environment; and the absolute requirement of intelligent tinkering is to save all the parts."

Aldo Leopold
American Forester, pioneer conserva-tionist and writer

Tourists also may pose a threat to mountain range habitats by damaging soil and vegetation through the great numbers of people. Volcanoes, geysers, waterfalls, canyons and glaciers are among the tourist attractions vulnerable to excessive numbers of people. Hunting is not permitted in National Parks and in Canada, but overuse of the more popular areas has steadily threatened and changed habitats in these places.

△ Edelweiss is a plant associated with the Alps. The true flower lies in the center of what looks like hairy white petals but are in fact leaves. Plants like these are endangered because they are being trampled or picked by tourists. In many parts of the Alps visitors have to keep to special trails to preserve the soil and the wildflowers.

▷ Before people and livestock could move into the Okavango Swamp, the area would have to be cleared of the tsetse fly which carries sleeping sickness. But spraying with insecticides not only detroys the fly, it is lethal to many birds, reptiles, small mammals and fish. It even destroys certain plants by killing their pollinators.

The wetlands

◁ The Okavango Swamp, is an 18,000 sq km (6,000 sq mi) floodplain in Botswana. The human population has increased so much that people west of the delta want to leave their overgrazed lands and move with their cattle into the delta proper. Plans have also been made to construct canals to carry water from Okavango to mining areas. These proposals could spell the end of Okavango as a wildlife sanctuary.

▽ Water birds abound in the Okavango floodplain. Resident birds include herons, spoonbills (seen in the photograph) and fish eagles. The swamps are also the wintering ground for large numbers of migratory ducks and geese.

All over the world wetlands are threatened by drainage and conversion to arable land. This has been encouraged by the mistaken idea that wetlands are wastelands. In fact they are a highly productive type of natural habitat. As well as producing quantities of fish, wildfowl and reeds, wetlands serve as natural reservoirs. They accumulate and store water in wet periods and release it during dry periods. Wetlands are also ideal bird sanctuaries because of the abundance of food and high level of security — marshy wetlands discourage four-footed predators. The Chesapeake Bay and the Okefenokee Swamp are examples of wetlands in the United States.

Internationally, wetlands are especially important for migratory birds. Turkey, for example, has about 10,000 sq km (3,900 sq mi) of wetlands which are important wintering areas for ducks, geese and other birds coming from breeding grounds on the Russian tundra. These wetlands are also stopovers for birds flying on to Africa.

Wasting our rivers and lakes

Many industries generate immense quantities of waste materials. Often the easiest way to get rid of these is to pour them into the nearest river. The Rhine, for instance, has been called Europe's main sewer.

Pollution has caused many rivers and lakes — including some of the Great Lakes — to become almost biologically dead. One of the best known examples is Lake Erie. For years sewage and industrial wastes, and large amounts of nitrates from fertilizers used on nearby agricultural land, were poured into the lake until it could no longer support life. But, after a 20-year-long struggle, the situation has improved dramatically.

> If the level of pollution in the Rhine continues unchanged and the cumulative burden thereby continues to rise, we fear that irrepairable damage to the entire North Sea ecosystem may be inevitable.
> Albert Prombst
> West German Research Ministry

An accident at a Swiss chemical plant in 1986 resulted in a large quantity of poisonous chemicals being poured into the Rhine. This pollution of Europe's waterways threatened neighboring countries through which the Rhine flows and was a major setback to the years of work which had gone into efforts to clean up this great river. The photograph shows eel killed by the spillage.

River estuaries, and, in tropical areas, mangrove swamps, are important habitats for many species of fish. The fish use them as spawning grounds and nurseries. But all over the world these aquatic habitats are being degraded or destroyed by industrial and agricultural pollution and the cutting of mangroves for fuel or building material. Dredging or filling in land to provide sites for buildings, roads and airports, for example, can have a devastating impact on both freshwater and coastal ecosystems. The construction of dams drowns the habitat of some species and blocks the passage of migratory fish such as the salmon.

▽ Pollution from a nearby industrial plant threatens Kenya's Lake Nakuru and its immense concentrations of flamingoes. These gatherings of thousands of flamingoes have been described as the finest bird spectacle in the world.

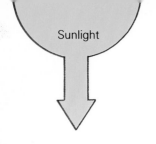

Sunlight

The ocean dump

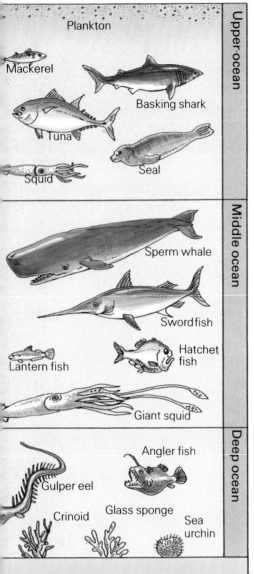

Upper ocean

Plankton

Mackerel

Basking shark

Tuna

Seal

Squid

Middle ocean

Sperm whale

Swordfish

Lantern fish

Hatchet fish

Giant squid

Deep ocean

Angler fish

Gulper eel

Crinoid

Glass sponge

Sea urchin

The seas have long been treated as the world's garbage dump, a convenient dumping ground for all kinds of waste materials. This did not matter too much until modern industry started generating quantities of poisonous wastes that were too dangerous to dispose of on land. After World War II, thousands of tons of unwanted poisonous gases, for example, were dumped at sea. More recently, the use of nuclear power plants has raised the problem of how to dispose of radioactive waste. Until recently the waste was sealed in special containers which, it was claimed, would be proof against corrosion until the contents stopped being radioactive. Then the containers were put into the sea.

Much of the pollution of the seas comes from crude oil. Each year millions of tons of crude oil are carried across the oceans by supertankers. Occasionally tankers are wrecked, causing serious pollution. But most pollution is caused by washing out the ship's tanks at sea. This is done to dispose of the unwanted residue after the cargo has been discharged – and totals several million tons a year. Some of this waste finishes up fouling beaches and shore lines and causes long-term problems for ocean wildlife.

△ Plankton forms the base of the ocean food chain. It supports large numbers of small fish. These are preyed upon by larger fish, which are in turn the prey of still larger fish. Waters beneath the surface are inhabited by free-swimming fish, squids and octopuses, sharks and rays, as well as whales and dolphins.

▷ Coral reefs are formed from the skeletons of millions of tiny creatures. They are complex communities of living creatures. These range from algae to shrimps and sea slugs, and from crabs, giant clams and octopuses to many types of brilliantly colored fish all in a balanced ecosystem. Coral formations all over the world are endangered by pollution as well as by removal of the coral for building material or for sale as tourist souvenirs. The photograph on the right contrasts a healthy reef with one that has been destroyed.

Islands - a delicate balance

The problems facing Mauritius are similar to those of many of the world's islands. When Europeans occupied Mauritius in 1598 they immediately began to exploit its natural wealth, especially the ebony forests. They brought with them goats, sheep and rabbits which destroyed the natural vegetation. Dogs and cats attacked the flightless birds such as the dodo; rats and pigs ate the eggs and hatchlings of ground-nesting birds, tortoises and turtles. Many species became extinct.

Today, Mauritius has one of the densest populations in the world. With little hope of finding employment or of leaving the island, the outlook for most of the islanders is bleak. Every available piece of land is cultivated: little of the natural habitat remains. And despite a world sugar surplus, great efforts are made to increase sugar production still more.

▽ The island of Madagascar contains plants and animals which are not found anywhere else. The aye-aye occurs only in Madagascar's rain forest. And with nine-tenths of its habitat already destroyed, it is one of the rarest animals in the world. In 1967, in an attempt to save the species from extinction, some of the last surviving aye-ayes were caught and released on the tiny uninhabited island of Nossi Mangabe, in the Bay of Antongil, where they are believed to be breeding satisfactorily.

Sugar cane plantations dominate the landscape in Mauritius. Sugar cane is easy to grow and is the mainstay of the island's economy. The only native woodlands remaining are a few isolated patches on the tops of hills. Flightless birds, such as the dodo, are characteristic of island faunas. But only one species has survived in the Indian Ocean – a flightless rail on Aldabra Atoll.

The development of commercial air routes has involved the building of airfields on previously inaccessible islands. Islands are also being used as satellite tracking stations, military bases and testing grounds for nuclear weapons. France has already carried out more than 80 nuclear tests in the Pacific. These developments, together with mass tourism and the widespread introduction of plantation crops such as sugar cane and coconut, have had catastrophic effects on many island habitats.

"Madagascar is a micro-cosm of the problems facing conservationists all over the world. The remaining wild areas represent an important part of the life support system for the human population as well as the wild species."

Lee Talbot
Director General
International Union
for the Conservation
of Nature and Natural
Resources

Price of progress

△ Following the country code helps to preserve the habitat.

The patchwork of small fields that forms a traditional country landscape is undergoing dramatic change. In England, for example, most of the chalk downland has been plowed. Ponds have been filled in and fens either drained or polluted with fertilizers. The process of converting small fields into large open spaces suitable for modern farming has destroyed a quarter of the country's hedgerows. Hedgerows form strips of natural habitat, making them havens for wild flowers, butterflies, birds such as the blackbird and robin, and small mammals like the hedgehog.

◁ In the spring toads migrate to their breeding ponds. Nothing — not even a highway — will stop them in their journey. Without specially built underpasses many would be killed by passing vehicles.

Industrial and other forms of development have had a major impact on the English landscape. Reservoirs and open-cast mining, electricity pylons and nuclear power stations, early warning systems and military training areas are some of the developments that have been imposed on the countryside. Rail and road networks, and especially highways, take up an enormous amount of land. Roadside verges, on the other hand, have a function similar to hedgerows and, for that matter, canal and river banks. They, too, serve as wildlife sanctuaries — as long as they are not sprayed with pesticides or herbicides.

The establishment of national parks is one of the main ways of preserving all types of natural habitat. In the United States and many other countries, development is carefully controlled to ensure that progress does not mean the degradation or destruction of habitat and wildlife.

△ The harvestmouse is just one of the many mammals affected by the changing countryside. Everyone can help preserve the countryside by observing the country code: always obtain permission before entering private land; keep to the footpaths and close all farm gates; avoid disturbing birds' nests or touching eggs. If you want to watch a nest, do so through binoculars from a distance; do not pick wild flowers: leave them for others to enjoy; take your litter home, and leave the countryside as tidy as you would like to find it.

Hard facts

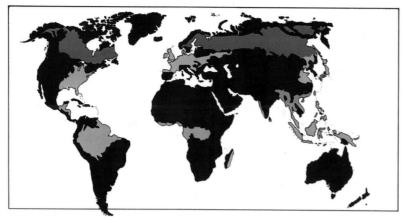

 Coniferous forest

Deciduous forest

Rain forest

Coniferous forests reach across North America and Eurasia; deciduous forests occur mainly in North America and Europe, and tropical rain forests mainly in Central and South America.

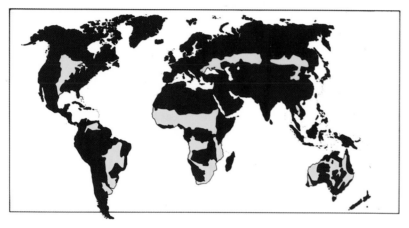

 Grasslands

The world's major grassland regions are the prairies of North America; the pampas and chaco of South America; the Eurasian steppes; and the African savannas. All have been exploited by humans.

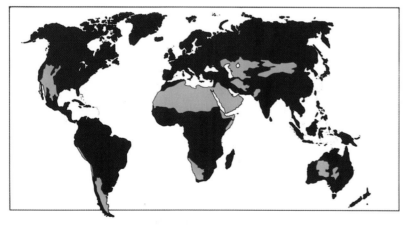

 Deserts

About one third of the world's land surface is desert. The largest and hottest is the Sahara, which occupies the greater part of northern Africa and forms part of a belt of arid lands extending across Asia to the Gobi in Mongolia.

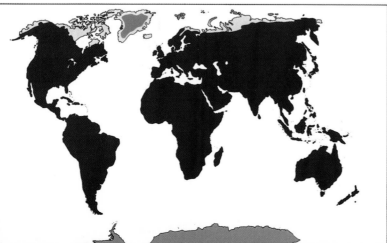

 Tundra

Ice caps

The Arctic is an ice-bound ocean. Antarctica is a continental land mass buried under ice. The tundra extends through northern Canada and the USSR.

Australia

A report by the government gives particulars of widespread and increasing damage to the environment. Two thirds of the country's tree cover has been destroyed; more than half the agricultural land is affected by soil erosion; and many rivers, wetlands and underground water sources badly degraded.

Brazil

Deforestation has reduced Brazil's Atlantic coastal forest to two per cent of its original size. This is the home of the golden lion marmoset, only about 400 of which survive.

Canada

Fears have been expressed that unless acid rain originating from industrial areas in the United States is effectively controlled, the country's maple trees will all be destroyed within 50 years.

Chile

The Juan Fernandez Islands, off the west coast of Chile, were the setting for the story of Robinson Crusoe. Of the 97 species of plants found only on this group of islands, more than half are under threat of extinction, arising from the introduction of goats, sheep, pigs and rabbits. Overgrazing has caused serious erosion: deep gullies are down to bedrock in many places.

China

The habitat of the giant panda in the forests of Sichuan has been seriously affected by timber extraction and grazing by domestic livestock. The Chinese authorities have taken a number of steps to safeguard the species, chief among them being the establishment of 12 special panda reserves totaling 6,000sq km (2,300 sq mi).

Indonesia

In an attempt to resolve its population problem the government is moving large numbers of people from the overcrowded islands of Java, Bali and Madura to the forests of Sumatra, Kalimantan and other outlying islands. This will inevitably be harmful to some of the most important tropical forests in the world.

Poland

The Bialowieza Forest, on the border between Poland and the USSR, is one of the last remaining areas of natural deciduous forest in Euorpe. It is the home of the only surviving herd of European bison, or wisent. At one time the wisent was widespread in the temperate forests of Europe. It is a woodland species and a browser, in contrast with the American bison which is a grazer. Wisent have also been reintroduced into the Caucasus.

Uganda

The mountain gorilla occupies a very restricted habitat in the mountains at the point where the borders of Zaire, Rwanda and Uganda meet. The forest habitat is constantly shrinking as more is taken over for growing crops, herding cattle and for wood cutting.

USSR

The USSR has set aside huge areas of land as nature reserves covering important types of ecosystems. Plans are being made to increase the number of reserves to include all the major types of habitat in the USSR.

United Kingdom

The merlin, Britain's smallest bird of prey, is endangered by pesticides in its food chain. Numbers (estimated at 600 pairs) are also falling because much of its moorland habitat is either being plowed to grow crops or planted with conifers.

United States

Atlantic salmon are reported to have returned to White River, Vermont, after an absence of many years. This follows a ten-year restoration program designed to improve the quality of the water and to instal fish ladders in dams. Salmon disappeared from New England rivers a century ago.

Index

Photographic Credits:
Cover and pages 7 (bottom) and 18-19: Survival Anglia; pages 4 (left) and back cover: Panos Pictures; pages 4 (right), 6, 7 (top), 8, 9 (top), 13, 17 (both), 20, 26 and 27: Bruce Coleman; pages 9 (bottom), 16, 17 (top) and 21: Zefa; pages 10-11 and 14: Spectrum; page 15: Frank Lane; page 19: Robert Harding; pages 23 (both) and 25: Planet Earth; page 24: John Hillelson Agency; page 28 (left): Guardian Newspaper; page 28-29: Hutchison Library; page 29: Tony Stone Associates.